Because a Fire
in Our Heads

Because a Fire
in Our Heads

Poems

Jay Udall

Texas Review Press
Huntsville, Texas

FIRST EDITION

Requests for permission to acknowledge material from the work should be sent to:

Permissions
Texas Review Press
English Department
Sam Houston State University
Huntsville, TX 77341-2146

Acknowledgments:

The author would like to thank the following publications, in which these poems first appeared, some in different forms:

Able Muse: "Tools of the Trade"; *Bayou*: "Leave-Taking"; *Beloit Poetry Journal*: "Because a Fire in Our Heads"; *Birmingham Poetry Review*: "Where It Begins"; *Cimarron Review*: "Blessing of the Beasts"; *Cincinnati Review*: "Exodus"; *Common Ground Review*: "Lost Feather, Little Wing" and "Outside"; *Cumberland River Review*: "Before Leaving"; *The Gulf Stream: Poems of the Gulf Coast* (anthology, Snake Nation Press): "To an Armadillo" and "Louisiana 1 South in Winter"; *Hawaii Pacific Review*: "The Hidden Grave"; *Iconoclast*: "For the Making"; *International Psychoanalysis*: "Timed Dive," "Company" and "What Returns"; *Kentucky Review*: "Meteor Shower," "Shhhh" and "To Feed the Feral"; *The Kerf*: "Sleeping with the Snake"; *Louisiana Literature*: "Passage" and "A Faltering Shelter"; *Minnesota Review*: "Jesus Walks in Blue above Louisiana"; *Miramar Poetry Journal*: "Void"; *North American Review*: "Sometimes a Bridge"; *The Pedestal*: "The Well Room"; *Prairie Schooner*: "Anonymous"; *Red Earth Review*: "Fledgling," "Reading Blind" and "Showing Forth"; *San Pedro River Review*: "Who Travels in the Ground," "Rest Area (No Facilities)" and "The Oracle at Amarillo"; *Spillway*: "Accompaniment," "Door in the Stone," "Embodied," "I Slip on a Pair of Water Moccasins," "Grief Songs" and "This Dirt Speaks"; *Superstition Review*: "Camerado" and "After the Murder of an Old Friend"; *The Swamp*: "Love Bugs"; *Yalobusha Review*: "The Rule of Attraction."

Cover art "Cabeza del Toro" by Rachel Udall

Cover design by Nancy Parsons, www.graphicdesigngroup.net

Library of Congress Cataloging-in-Publication Data

Names: Udall, Jay, 1959- author.
Title: Because a fire in our heads : poems / Jay Udall.
Description: First edition. | Huntsville, Texas : Texas Review Press, [2018]
  | Includes bibliographical references. |
Identifiers: LCCN 2018002045 (print) | LCCN 2018005179 (ebook) | ISBN
  9781680031515 (ebook) | ISBN 9781680031508 | ISBN 9781680031508¬q(pbk.)
Subjects: LCSH: Desire--Poetry.
Classification: LCC PS3621.D35 (ebook) | LCC PS3621.D35 A6 2018 (print) | DDC
  811/.6--dc23
LC record available at https://lccn.loc.gov/2018002045

I went out to the hazel wood,
Because a fire was in my head . . .

—W.B. Yeats

Contents

V. What Returns

Because a Fire
in Our Heads

I. Because a Fire in Our Heads

*I've often lost myself, in order to find
the burning that keeps everything awake.*
—Federico Garcia Lorca

The Well Room

Lift the old board and a coolness
shaped like the inside would rise
with the held-in smell of rust, webs, wet
cinderblock and earth, many-legged lives
thriving in the blind black, forgotten
hollow that thumped like a drum under
our bare or sneakered or snow-booted feet,
in the very center of our yard, beneath
kick-the-can and hide-and-seek, below
our noise, drama, schemes: another room.
It housed a pump that pulled water from deep
ground to our faucets. In my head it drank
from the river down the cliff where we caught
catfish, bass and eel and threw the eel back
but dark-skinned men sliced them into pieces
to bait hooks, blood redder than our own blotching
the sun-warmed concrete beside the spillway
that swallowed boys who tried to run it in tubes.
Trees, stars reached from places no eye could see.
A lame dog and a sick friend disappeared.
Once, to be as brave as my brother, I crouched
in that squat hole as he pulled the board over,
the bright summer day and all that was in it
drifting too easily away without me.
When the pump failed, our father would lower
himself in, stooping to the work, cursing, rising
to search his tool chest for a different wrench, the one
that would bring the water back, the top of him
sticking out of the mouth, going down again.

Because a Fire in Our Heads

The leash yanks—a trace, invisible
messages trailing

I open a book, seeking
a remembered passage

as far down the scale of life as the worms and even perhaps
to the amoebas, we meet a general alertness of animals,
not directed toward any specific satisfaction, but merely
exploring what is there; an urge to achieve intellectual
control over the situations confronting them

grackles cackle in the bamboo

*

suspended from nothing, pennants
of breathing white putty hovered
above our heads, one for each,
pursuing us wherever we ran
in the green field—dread

*

when the blood vessel broke in the left brain
of the neuroscientist, she couldn't say
where she ended and universe began—
it was all a matter of energy
shimmering swim of molecules atoms
streaming fabric of being belonging
her tears recalled when she could speak again,
out of her right mind, trying to explain
to the hungry brains gathered in the hall
what she'd seen and touched on the other side

*

the seeking circuit fires during the search for food,
not during the final locating and eating of the food.
It's the search that feels so good

*

in a dream I vomit up
living fish—
the river, somewhere close

*

words shaping air, stroking skins
(braided bark, old scar) awake

in the mind flesh flames
with rustlings of switchgrass,

crow caws, purple starflower
and fire ants, the quiet cow

come to the killing floor,
the body a story being
told, untold tongues telling

*

inside: spin and pull,
whirled space of muons
and bosons, weak force, strong force,
quarks named "strange" and "charm"

dark energy, dark matter

outside: this cosmos
one among many

lifeless or haunted
by life forms, seeking

                    *

say nothing
say no one
is ever lost
forever lost
say what slips
from saying
what is said
by "this leaf"
or "the rain"
say the names
we can't keep
what keeps us

                    *

absconded gods,
Ithaca, Eldorado,
ghosts of appetite—

say emptiness
is an entrance,
disorderly ditch
of pungent mud and slime,
last year's tattered cattails,
new reed blades rising,
not the singing
of a golden bird
on a golden bough,
but trills and raspy clicks
of red-winged blackbirds
in the accidental light.

Accompaniment

Comes the dishwasher's face
scoured by exhaustion
as he slogs out the back door
at day's end, down a concrete path
strewn with tubes and slurries
of goose crap, past the geese
gliding the pond's inverse sky,
I press my hand to the wall, feel
the soft screeching of hatchlings inside.
Come the dwarf women trying to get in
my glass door, a three-legged dog lies
down in my bed, a lion walks through
my fear, I hear in the vents feral cries,
hushed utterances, time falling
through the faces of dead friends.
Come the voices speaking
in my voice, in these words
as I say them, or they say me.
Comes no one again, peering in the windows.
Comes the one who grins at destruction,
the one who stays young in the shadows.
Come the fresh scars, the buried eyes,
a man with no arms smoking
a cigarette with his toes,
moonlight a minute old,
Lady Day unhinging the air.

Fledgling

Stranded, flown too soon
from branches above
where parents scream out
in helpless safety
as I approach,
a small black bird quivers
in a green expanse.
Looking up, it seems
still stunned by its fall
into this new view,
this towering thing
stopping, looking down.

I'm a boy, watching
a friend, his father dead,
turn a lighter and a can
of hairspray into a blowtorch
to blaze a city of ants.

I'm thirteen, too much alone
with too many deaths,
a savage voice rising
in my throat as I chase
a dog, throwing rocks
to fill it with fear,
to stop my own fear
from feeding on me.
I'm a pair of pants,
a shirt, shoes, nothing
under looming blue.

*

Once, stopped on the way
to see my dying mother,
I watched five kittens
play in a dry wash
of red rock, red sand,
scrub willows, mean heat,
their mother gone for food
or gone for good,
and thought of my child
not yet three months old
sleeping with her mother
back in the cooled dark
of a motel room,
how much she needed
us just to survive,
while some of those strays,
even on their own,
would likely scavenge by.

*

Oppenheimer watching
the first flash and bloom
of a thousand suns,
vision of godly force
in human hands made real,
the invisible heart
of matter split to
melt cities, foreign flesh:
Now I am become Death,
the Destroyer of worlds.

*

Night comes, bodies curl
to one another, cities
cling to Earth's curves, careless
Mother who breathes us,
leaves us to our own.

O blessed rage for power—
on every side pure
space keeps opening.
The world is flying.

Timed Dive

My brother keeps diving down through blue
to crouch on the bottom in a corner of the deep end
and hold his breath as long as he can, timing himself
with the diver's watch he got one summer
of steel bands, coral reefs, painted fish.
He stays down there longer and longer. I swim
and swim until I tire of it, then sit in a sunny chair,
watching him as he studies his watch with the same
blank face he's worn since coming back,
black sunglasses still hiding his eyes,
his near silence now complete inside the water.
Nine years old, I just want to go home.
He's come back to say goodbye
before leaving for the war. He's leaving,
crossing the border into Canada, sinking
alone where he can't say, mouth filling
with black, breathing it as he falls
through, watching his mirrored eyes spin,
no ladder back, no sides, no bottom.
With a different name he's returning
to our distances, trying to kill himself
by driving off a bridge, surviving
to hear the court martial judge pronounce
him a disgrace to family and nation,
he's shattering our windows with his boots
and fists, screaming in a locked bathroom
he wants to cut off his cock, taking the pills
they say will help him, but he won't come
up, we won't get home. I rise from my chair,
turn to leave, I dive where I can't see,
I reach and reach.

Tools of the Trade

It was tough killing each other with stones.
I mean, if you could catch a guy sleeping
you'd just drop a big one on his head, but
more often he'd spot you lugging that thing
his way, and run. Then someone realized
a spear was good for more than hunting, though
issues with distance and running remained
until addressed by the speed and piercing
precision of an arrow's tip let go
from a string of hide stretched tight—such quiet
dread whole armies rained on each other's heads.
Yet I confess nostalgia for the knife,
a hand-spear with facets of surprise and
intimacy. You had to look a guy
in the eyes or, if you chose to backstab,
firmly clasp one shoulder with your free hand
in an almost brotherly way to slip
the blade in deep—shades of Abel and Cane,
family business, a living tradition.
Guns? Invented by cowards. Any fool
can kill, and the poor victim might as well
be an *idea*, for god's sake, a distant
abstraction, even more so when you drop
a bomb from the sky like some kind of god,
even worse when you press a button, launch
a missile or drone, turn away to play
eighteen holes. Where's the sport in *that,* the warmth
and humanity, so far and so clean—
where's the murderer in the machine?

The Hidden Grave

The someone we killed,
my cousin and I
in our youth, a face
I can't see, but weak
and dumb—he was ours,
the air become red,
limbs and head severed
to move in the dark
to some hidden grave,
though each place we thought
seemed to scream our guilt
as if some magic
pact with the soil we
had broken and lost.

Finally the fact
sealed in our silence,
all traces erased,
the earth-dragging weight
blood-lugged as we stepped
back into our lives,
our selves, somebody
else's flesh masks fixed
in place, until I
woke in a world where
no one was missing
because of us, me,
absolved by light, free,
a clean emptiness.

But who did I kill
and bury inside?

Seen

after Laurens van der Post

He said his eyes would always see that
morning in the camp when their captors
made them stand at attention in neat rows
to watch a friend be tortured, executed.

Their ears could not escape his screaming,
but no one could force them to watch
the knife slicing his bare torso, the slow
blood, his clawed face, eyes.

He said his eyes found the jungle floor, slipped
inside red-black space, as if to save him,
but a voice—where did it come from?—said
No. You must watch. You must watch—for him.

A Certain Confusion

for the White Helmets of Syria

For so long they had pulled so many dead
and alive from so many different piles
of rubble, different days, different bombings,
there came to some a certain confusion.

One, rescuing an infant still breathing,
was sure he was saving his own daughter.
Another, hearing of a bombing near home,
worried about his son. When word finally came

the boy was safe, he rejoiced, then thought of all
the others now buried beneath their buildings.
"But really," he said, "what's the difference
between my child and another person's?"

They had seen and done too much. Bombs kept falling
and who could blame them for losing their sense?

Camerado

Two strangers, men, sitting side by side,
traveling through a terror-stricken time,
we are suddenly embarrassed to find
that for many minutes unnoticed
our legs have been pressed together,
enjoying the animal warmth
of their surreptitious contact.

Lick and Stroke

Galway Kinnell, in memoriam

Lit windows float in the night stream

the distances between familial stars

to point, to signal, in time: these hands: words

to lick and stroke the world

the man spoke and the silence took him in

the way light sometimes touches, a voice, skin.

Head Massage

You love when I massage your scalp,
even this fault line, long-healed scar
where the surgeons parted your skull
to pull the tumor out.

When the ground gave way I pitched through
tumbling down starless black grasping
at the soft furniture of nothingness
as I sat in a chair with magazines,
or talked and ate at a table with friends,
or walked the sun-filled street,
my feet slowly given back by what
I might have only imagined
out of pure lack—nothing
but a buoyancy from nowhere
lifting, some gravity pulling up.

And here you are, seated before me
on the floor, facing away,
offering your head to my hands,
saved by some convergence
of skill and luck, still arriving
in the open-ended air.
How could I ever imagine
you? But I must, again and again, if
I'm ever to reach you, these fingers
sifting your flora, reading the terrain,
this rift in your planet's plates.

Outside

Half a day after a tsunami hits Japan
surging waves arrive on the shores
of northern California.
Two hundred miles inland, in jagged winds
our daughter pretends to be a dragon.
Online you can view satellite images of before—
green neighborhoods, business districts, industrial sites—
then click to see barren gray ground after,
destruction unearthing the spirits
of Hiroshima and Nagasaki,
radiation plume shape-shifting
its way across the Pacific.
In the aftershock that lasts, the faces
clad in surgical masks, eyes stripped to survival.
One man scoops rice by hand from open ground
where, hours before, his kitchen enclosed him.
His boat gone, a fisherman says, "I don't know
what we did for God to do this to us."
Bodies float, wash up with boards, cars, trees.
The missing are their own city.

*

In the minute of our only earthquake
we were still waking, slowly entering
a clear spring morning, when the shaking came
through us, through the walls, the floor
we rode as we tried to brace, thrown
outside, where there was no more outside,
while Rachel slept on in her room.

*

I tell Rachel that Japan fell two feet, slid
this way thirteen, but leave out the part about
the planet getting knocked ten inches off axis,
the daily counting of the killed and lost.
Yet the way she asks about meteors
slamming Earth, I suspect she already knows
our predicament, the way the body
remembers in certain moments
how we turn and float in shorelessness.

On a blanket in a gymnasium,
surrounded by hundreds of displaced others,
a girl and an old man play a game of Go,
making a momentary room.

Extreme Home Makeover

It was some kind of paralysis
or death-wish, denial, bad dream
I would wake from to find the world
as always, as if guaranteed
by my gods, my glowing screens.
                              In another room
skyscraper ice sheets were plunging
to ocean, coral gardens
blanching to bone, the old floor
falling, animals vanishing.
                              I reached
for the switch in the dark—
                              the wall—

II. Blessings of the Beasts

*One does not meet oneself until one catches
the reflection from an eye other than human.*
—Loren Eiseley

The Following Tiger

When I felt my life fading, he appeared

in every room of that dream I entered,
padding softly, silently through the halls,

a ghost, real, electric where he walked.

I thought if I ignored him, kept moving
I'd escape notice, but when I laid down

on the floor, spent, he laid beside me, stretched

his thick neck, his great head, across my chest.
I kept still under that thrumming then felt

him melt into me, the current coursing.

Blessing of the Beasts

Let it rise from the windowless houses
in which chickens sit their entire brief lives
in darkness, wing to wing, breasts bred so
heavy they struggle to walk, stop trying.
Let it lift them into confused light
with the matted grasses and blackened leaves
below the field of ice where I blow
on cold coals in a pit of ash and bone.
Let it come from the calcium veins
branching under graveyards, be root-sucked
into breathing green, feed, flower this brain
to see through the city's magic mirrors
the earth snake's eyes peering in and out.
Not the immaculate Mind purified
of death, but blessings of skin, scale, fur
and feather, breath and pulse, the old blood,
the code kept and spoken from the first cell
saying *trilobite, chameleon, gray wolf,*
the chimera we name *the self,*
chatter, warble, growl, shriek, moan.
For the sparks and flashes, skull skies, temples
of piss and shit, ancestral spirits, gods
crawling, clawing, tunneling, flying,
tasting clouds, oceans, soils, sun in seeds,
muscles, pulps, leaves, saps, oils, juices,
the tongue circling the tender center,
mouth enfolding, stroking the veined stalk,
for the burst, thrust, outrush of fire and space
becoming, and the counter-pull, the gathering
attraction, slow accretion of matter
remembering in this trembling, this singing,
this dying, this dreaming meat.

Door in the Stone

Under the red ochre and charcoal deer
whose antlers branch up and up like trees
ready for leaves and birds and further shining,
under the extinct steppe bison, the horses,
goats, the hands floating on ceilings and walls,
you can make out earlier versions
as fine or finer, faded, still vivid, as if
later hands had been drawn to try themselves,
working by mind's eye and fire's rhythms far
inside the dense dark—was there chanting? dancing?—
to form the figures that spark and quicken.
As if the object was not the object
but a door in the stone—what could open
through our fingers, what might branch from our heads.

The Rule of Attraction

Don't kick the rattlesnakes! Now you've done it—
they're circling you, the not-snake among them.
Now Thelonius Monk rises
from his piano, begins spinning,
leaves the stage—and the stage follows.
Thunder comes through the clear walls
and a bug with an orange triangle
for a back travels the kitchen sink's lip,
the world passing through us as we pass
in electromagnetic push-pull.
Near and far, bodies bend space, alluring,
while the Giant watches without eyes,
with eyes of blue fire, dull white, black.
But how did you and the snakes change
into--raccoons, are you? I see you see
me, you leap from the circle and run
this way, my human daughter.

Love Bugs

So named in jest for how they're going
at it, hooked up good, back to back, riding
each other through surging late summer heat
when they come in black storms swirling,
spattering our windshields, thick sticky
whitish blood glazing the glass, and now
we see only darkly, but don't we feel
some semblance of ourselves, our own desire,
whirling blindly back at us, spending itself
so cheaply and prodigiously? *Is this love?*
as Bob Marley asks, and if not, then where
is the line between, finer than this sheet
of super-heated, clarified sand that stands
between us and what's out there, a ghostly
demarcation somewhere in the mind, find
it on the MRI, *Where is the love?*—
not the locus lit up in valentine red,
but the thing itself, no thing but a kind
or quality of feeling, a certain mode
of being and doing, what we give and take
as human yet something of a hand-me-down
from our mammalian great-great-great grandfolks
out of which we fashion this garment of
our own, growing into its shape and size.
Pick a thread, unravel the fabric, follow
it back down the spiraling stairs to chat
with the mitochondria, those familial strangers
powering our castles from inside each cell,
the acidophilus claiming squatter's rights
in our gut tunnels, the flu bug finding
our lips, French-kissing our warm wet mouths.
Ask them all if they don't love us wildly,
fiercely, for life, as these other bugs love
each other unto death, into juice
smeared under our wipers as we peer through
the carnal carnage and drive on, driven
by our loves.

Embodied

Morning: a dead doe in the median.
Here the woods are small islands we've left
to rabbit, fox, deer.

At dusk they sometimes come to the edges,
coats colored like the wet winter trees
they vanish back into

as if to remind the mind
what it is—momentary
animal eye gazing

out from long branchings
of blood, eyes in limbs
and skin, the earthly host.

                    *

My dog stops in the dark
as if he sees, among
stripped boughs, something

where there is nothing,
but something—shadow
glowing, shape

of doe.

Passengers

Martha, the last passenger pigeon, died September 1, 1914
in captivity, where she had lived all of her twenty-nine years.

Stuffed feather bag with carmine eyes of glass,
severed branch. She came too late to belong
to the biblical droves that dimmed our sun
for days passing over, whirling masses
that made us believe there could be no end
to their kind, a bounty poured from God's hand.
We slaughtered more than we could ever eat,
killing to know the power in our hands
that said we too were deathless, infinite.
Then woke to what was left, what had left us.

Before the Harvest

Cane field stirs with wind, other presences.
Between late October's rows you can see

in only a few feet—then shadow
night deep at noon, house of many rooms, quiet

of copperhead, fox, rabbit. mice, peace breathing
between sudden terrors, quick deaths. Not yet

the rumbling underneath, the roar-whine
approaching, rustles turned to panicked rush

bolting from nest and shelter into
naked light, a crouching sky, scurrying

for any uncertain cover—exodus
of Earth's latest refugees. Not yet

the lush columns cut to stubble, dirt burnt,
sweetness in cup and bowl for distant tongues.

Now belongs to crickets praising
the god of evening, to the swallows

arriving to sweep the animate air,
to all thriving in the spaces between.

Snakes and Tortoise

My dream snake slides loose
up a cinderblock wall

to fight another snake
on a tin roof—the two

multiply—a tangle
of coils biting, writhing

on another roof
a large tortoise tries

to climb away, snakes
stabbing its neck and legs

from every side
I want him to pull in

shut his shell, save himself
if he can, but he can't

or won't, as if he thinks
his only chance is

to reach the roof's peak
where he'll swim into sky

I'm biting, and bit.

To Feed the Feral

Greenish gold eyes frame me: threat.
How long did it take to break
the trust of ten thousand years?
She carries mute history,
her coat a genetic mash-up
of gray and orange patches,
dab of white on striped tail.
Is she wrong to fear this hand
that belongs to the kind who murder
their own in schools and churches?
Yet need draws us near,
though our hungers may differ.
I step softly, bringing bowls
of slaughtered fish, slowly hold
out my fingers to be sniffed.
She basks in sun-warmed grass
in this small piece of yard,
and long before she allows me
to stroke her neck, shoulders, back,
skin begins to gentle fur
as fur gentles skin.

To an Armadillo

You're one I can't count
on—you're a promise
never made, sometimes kept

when you surreptitiously
tiptoe down summer
night streets between, under

parked cars, through ditches
and culverts, behind bush
and brush, with that head

you might have stolen from
some newborn kangaroo,
long ears like curled leaves,

tapered snout that sees
for feeble eyes any
ant or beetle, any

subterranean grub
or root, any tossed
scrap of fruit or half-

eaten hamburger
half-wrapped, waiting
in some gutter.

In hard light I've seen
on roadsides that same armor
crushed by rushing steel tons,

corpses so common they blind
us to your prehistoric
glory, your nine plates

gates into another
story of the body
in the book of Earth,

your untamed flame venturing
through the large darkness,
returning the night.

Sleeping with the Snake

All night he curled by my legs
like a kitten or dog.
Dreaming inside a dream
I could vaguely feel
something against my calf,
but didn't think of scaled skin.

I woke with his leaving
then woke again, my fear
baffled that he hadn't harmed me,
had only wanted to rest
in the heat my body gave.

Lost Feather, Little Wing

*. . . no one will deny that there is
at least some roughness everywhere.
—Benoit Mandelbrot*

Six stripes reached across like ink
bleeding through a paper bag—
no question of perfection
but a quick draft, sloppy copy,
the chestnut lines that broke
up into something between
brown and *orange*, not *red*
(though color is in eye and light,
they say, not in the thing itself).
At first look the underside flashed
silver-white, fascia hugging muscle
not there, a faint iridescence
and then, close below, profuse flecks
of cerulean, patches of sky.
Tightly packed tines turned to kitten fur
at the edges where bird swept air.
I was driving home when it lifted
from the passenger's seat and flew
out an open window.

Showing Forth

In a field left for less than worthless
below the highway's headlong tide,
from barren ground more rock and sand than soil,
from thirst inside of thirst, they rise
in green: smallest fingers, claws, spiders spreading.

*

Thread-veins curl off the hard nub and spine
of a maple seed's single wing,
bending back like stroked hair,
supple yellow-green membrane thinning
to transparence, turning the faintest
tinged-with-blood red, stuck in between
the tread of a truck's motionless tire—
falling, flying.

*

After heavy summer rains they appear
by the path, chest high, a great crowd, crimson
shot through stalks and branches—bodies stripped
of skin, fat, tendon, bone—arterial
beasts born of seed and dust, spirits
of matter, inside out.

The Gathering

They're coming, already here
climbing out of enclosing ocean

echoing cave on two legs, four
more, none, gnawing rock, sun

one another, they rise through
sperm and ovum, axon and dendrite

through words, circuits, fields of air
crossing savanna and tundra, blind

corridors, long bridges dissolving
following, carried along in shadows

blooming inside our sleep, with a skull
for a drum, with a flickering lamp

bringing beast and blessing they set
the table and make themselves the feast

they pull out the chairs, scraping
the scarred floors, they put a fork

in my hand, a knife in yours.

III. Leave-Taking

Before Leaving

He had walked down the leafed tunnel as if
he meant to do something in the minutes
before he would go. He might have carried
a shovel or rake, his hard, splintered skin
curled to smooth handle, but he stopped before
the gate, stood there, seemed to lose himself in
gazing out where a sorrel horse ambled
through light, trees shimmered in wind. He forgot
his purpose, or felt it falter, go out,
stranding him in between, and maybe this
was why he'd come back, without knowing it,
to let himself be filled with what he saw
while he still could. It was all already
leaving, going on without him—

Shhhh

My mother is blowing gently in my ear
to make a soft place for me to sleep
inside my pain. If she stops a moment
too long I wake in its clench,

                              Being, but an Ear

in a dark motel room somewhere
in Arizona, traveling somewhere
I no longer believe in.

And what could I do for her
in her final pain, but kiss the bones
rising through her hands and face
and listen, as I listen now,
for something back of all that is
and isn't said—a gate between
breaths, a path in air.

Company

The dying man sat among us
as we talked of the weather,
politics, ourselves, waiting
 for the turkey and the ham,
though sometimes we remembered
to draw him in, a near stranger
invited to share Easter,
no one else to have him.
He smiled and asked for red wine,
filled his plate, ate better
 than he had in weeks, he said,
then fell asleep in the passenger's seat,
his head leaning on my shoulder
as I drove him to his empty house.

Three nights before my mother died
she made us carry her out to the living room
to visit with those who had gathered.
Exhausted from pain, dreaming on morphine,
she kept falling asleep, we kept pleading,
Don't you want to go back to bed and rest?
Her eyes, voice went knife-clear:
"No. Not with such good company."
The Hostess, the way she'd always lived
for other people, through other people.
But the next day, starting to shed her
self like a worn-out dress, she said,
"Maybe next time we'll each have our own
galaxies. We could visit now and then.
But all of you are a bit much."

Leave-Taking

Father, leave your books and papers, your glasses
on the desk. Leave your wallet on the dresser,
the pictures on the walls. Leave the walls.

Leave your clothes in the closet still
bearing your scent, the ghost of your shape.
Leave in your favorite green corduroys

with the fraying waist and cuffs
and the gaudy bathrobe you loved
for some reason we'll never quite know.

Leave your view of the mountains
framing the passing sky,
the *optical delusion*

of your separateness, your dreaming I,

the unframed threshold where we breathe.

Reading Blind

The history of my gathering blindness begins
as I close the back cover of some children's novel
and wake, alone, my family far in sleep,
deep night pressing against the windows, claiming all
but the circle of light around my lamp and bed.
Then I'm poring through Schopenhauer,
Leviticus, Dickinson—ghosted thoughts,
hours, ages pouring through me, my body going
stiff and numb as some abstraction or the chair
in which it sits, eyes tracking the lines
as if one of these times I might see through
the words, the shapes of letters, through ink
and pulp, inside the echoing orbits
of charged particles, into the womb
of speech—to be spoken—flesh
become word, breath, first and final silence.
Years slip, I slip into bed beside my sleeping wife,
a hive of ideas swarming behind my burning lids
until daybreak, gray light too bright,
our daughter gnawing the spines of her first books.
My father looks at us with raw wounds
in his sockets from his merciless hunger
for illumination, a shimmering half
remembered, half unseen, the light of one eye
giving way to shadow shapes, our forms
trading names on his lips as he goes, letting go
of syllables, saying less than he sees, seeing
less than he knows, slipping through these lines
to vanish. An orange and white traffic barrel
becomes a man in a striped shirt. A woman appears
to tenderly embrace a trash can. My eyes
close and some partial face gazes out
through sleep's shredding walls, reading me,
as fish that look like fingers see without eyes
lightless lakes somewhere below Kentucky,
as I read the dark, feeling my way.

Grief Songs

Rabbit eyes—black stones—stare from the gutter.
Loosening, its coat sags, ripples, an empty shirt.
Night wakes me in its skin, stripped of desire.

*

A snake flies to the sun,
finds its hungry egg,
stars showering down through
purple, magenta, long tails
writhing as they drift
like ash through air turned black.

*

In a room of earth—
but I'm room, earth—
sharp-beaked birds spiral
up an invisible pole
toward a pinhole of blue.
My chest, head break open
and bats scatter.

*

Grass keeps growing out of a man's head.
Who is the seed in its pod blessed
by flames like hands, or hands like flames?
A boat is going and coming,
the river changing languages.
Green are my tears
and green is death.

For the Making

Seamus Heaney, in memoriam

The spade-pen is still. Given note, voice, song—
they've stopped in his throat. Those hard consonants
opened Irish ground, seeking their source, found
the bottomless centre and bog goddess,
her kept corpses, sacrifice, blood justice,
old death-lust he refused, imagining
a city barely seen, a happening
at eye's edge where buried shard meets birth light,
becomes a vessel housing breath. Ample
make his bed: what he sounded receives us.
A roped bucket drops through blind echoings,
a thirst taking the dark's shape, shaping it
into words to wake the world to itself,
the living work, the thick and quick of it.

Anonymous

Was that you sitting on the bench, watching
the pond, the hill greening with weeds?
When I looked back, you were walking away, slowly,
as if waiting for someone to catch up.
If that wasn't you, then who was seated
beside me last night in a dream, cursing
the purest white, soft-soled, slip-on shoes
we all had to wear in our prison?
I slip on someone else's thrift store skin
and my stories rearrange, changing colors.
A chrysalis opens, I look up through
my father's dying eyes, sinking away
from familiar voices fading and blending,
drifting toward the mouths of fire, dirt, air.

Fish wander the pond's body opened by light.
The earth breeds pinks, yellows, purples as
something breathes me and my hand reaches again
for the meat, the wine. What I meant to ask was,
Who or what is gazing through our eyes?

The Further Definition

But she must have been very beautiful
at the end, wrote my senior friend, hearing
of my mother's death at seventy-nine.
Beautiful? I thought to say. *Beautiful*

how cancer had carved her to sharp angles,
the skull pressing through her face, bewildered
eyes looking out from and into a place
beyond our seeing? Beautiful the young

couple coupling I once stumbled upon
in woods beside a quick stream. Beautiful
to recall loving with my bride-to-be
in the woods beside a stream. *Beautiful*

the tributaries now etching her face
toward that invisible ocean? *Beautiful*
the fine reddish blue veins spreading like slow
lightning strikes across my ankles and legs?

Who was I to quail when trying to help
my father put in his new dental bridge
and glimpsing the charred ruins of his teeth?
Only air where he stood. Beautiful flames.

Who Travels in the Ground

On knees, clawing dirt
clumps to loosen roots
thick as arteries, tangled
sinews, fine hairs clinging
to bits of seashell, bone
chips, soil slick and pliant
underneath—Louisiana
loam still strange to my hands,
pulling the light in
as it's turned, folding
back into itself, smearing
shovel, shoes, skin.

I remember us, old man,
years back one spring
morning in New Mexico
carving holes in *caliche*
to put in purple ice plant,
coreopsis, firewheels—
crops for craving eyes
in the high desert,
sun so close I feel it
searing arms and neck
but can't make myself break
the intimate rhythm
that carries us
in our silence,
shovels and trowels
clanging, scraping, rasping
against rock and sand,
trying to chisel out
room enough for roots
to seek and take hold, feed
blossoms from the dark.

How can we say we love the Earth
unless we learn to greet death,
this ground that eats each body
in time, this perishing flesh
you clothed me in
out of yourselves dreaming
awake as you fell
toward the silence
I'm digging inside—
my work, my fear
and hunger, my violence.

Good to find you here.
Forgive me my wanderings
as I let your absences go,
as I clear the bed
for the reaching down,
the slow rising and swelling
of skins with meats, juices, seeds
we'll bring to our mouths
a thousand miles from where
we freed your dust.

IV. Traveling Here

The miracle is not to walk on water or fire.
The miracle is to walk on the earth.
—Linji Yixuan

Sometimes a Bridge

You can't see it because you're riding
in the passenger's seat, but I'm driving
with my left eye closed. Don't look like that—
it's okay. I see things better this way
when I'm this stoned. "It's not a bad pitch
if I can hit it," said Roberto Clemente.
Look. Remember? That park with flowing hills
and secretive trees is where you lost your virginity
to a girl whose adopted father beat her.
For a while in your arms she was happy.
Or were you the girl? Or the father?
When I open my eye the world doubles
and I can't always tell which one's real.
"Convergence strabismus," the doctor said,
meaning I look at things closer than they are.
If I reached for your arm my fingertips
 might brush ghosted air. On this corner
they severed your head, propped it
on your corpse to be a word of God.
Now I'm the silence into which you spoke,
though I might have been laughing then, splashing
with my young daughter a few worlds away.
Sometimes a bridge--like this one,
steep air bristling with messages,
lustrous waves pulsing below.
Here, you drive.

Exodus

It is kind of the ceramic frog
to seem to stay where it is
day after day in the backyard. Likewise

the backyard. Likewise this window
that looks and looks and looks out there.
Here's to the brass knob and the brown door

entering morning. Here's to the hinges,
to the screws holding the hinges,
old wood holding screws,

the fast foundation sliding
where we pour and pour hot tar
into cracks in the fractured asphalt

gripping the archaic ground crawling
where branches reach through themselves,
air sheds its skin and sidewalk steps

toward each death, all the worlds unfolding—

Rest Area (No Facilities)

An open room owned by wind,
metal roof blistering turquoise

in between in between far places
cars (silhouettes of climate-controlled heads) blur

to and from and to, escaping a slow
avalanche of light that smothers all color.

Stunted weeds, scattered rocks that enter
no one's thoughts or calculations. How many years

since someone stopped here? Even ants
are absent. We piss behind twisted cedars,

eat apples and plums on a cement bench,
our words quickly killed by the wide dry air,

throw pits and cores that will not take.
Sixteen minutes and we're chased away,

 back inside our songs and stories,
our faces vivid, laughing,

that immense emptiness
waiting somewhere ahead.

Passage

for Rachel

Pulled along in the rush of cars
crossing a bridge through coming dark,
she saw in the trees lining the river
litter scattered—sheets and sheets
of crumpled paper or plastic grocery bags
swept up there by some fierce wind—
a shuddering, flapping, folding
of *wings*—*birds*, they were birds
gathered in the branches to sleep
as night drew sky and trees and river
into its cave—she could still see them
glowing in the opened walls
long after she'd forgotten where
she was going, what she'd wanted to reach.

Traveling Here

Should we have stayed at home,
wherever that may be?
—Elizabeth Bishop

Some emperor has spread his gray robe
over all. Gray waters seep to gray oceans,
contours of interred pain, tender flesh
inside a crustacean's claw.
I watch through the random windows
assigned to me: trees being shaken by wind,
a single bird making its way somewhere,
and a small patch of furry weeds (lamb's ears?)
grows in. Storied leaves clack and trill above.
I remember lion-headed monkeys,
the end--beginning?--of the rainbow that walked
down the street to pass two feet from our parked car
as we sat inside, waiting out the storm.

Love, where are we? This now is almost
too much, all we have, all we've ever had.
The ringing of hidden crickets rises
from under rabbit brush, clusters of bright yellow
blossoms breathing brighter in leaving light
before fading inside the ash of dusk.

The Oracle at Amarillo

Find the motel laundry room,
the one windowsill
smudged with ash and charred butts,
coffee stains and feedlot dust.

Listen through highway sighs,
gazing at the empty parking lot,
the fence shedding its brown paint,
and what's left of the sky.

All questions will be answered.

I Slip on a Pair of Water Moccasins

and tread where the dead float in white rooms
bearing crosses above the rot, unrooted
as Spanish moss riding deathless branches,
gorging on light as I gnaw death and the light
in death, I know why my dog barks at Jesus
statues in the dark and why our black neighbors
pretend we're not here, history is the thick
wet heat, skin we're in, mosquito sting
and dragonfly iridescence, fractal eye,
Fats walking to New Orleans as bullets
sing in the corpses of black cane workers,
Thibodaux gotta go me oh my oh
across the Huey Long Bridge, Big Muddy
pouring America's poisoned waters,
Jim and Huck drifting free on their wide raft,
we rise as we drown, carry ground layered
with seashells remembering a salt sky
and what carries us, armless, uncarried,
the land vanishing from under as
we step second line through the eyewall.

Strike and Harvest

One of the most interesting, and probably least known,
events in Louisiana history is the Thibodaux Massacre,
the second most bloody labor dispute in U.S. history.
Strikers and their family members were rounded up by
vigilantes. Many were told to "run for their lives"
before being summarily executed. On the morning of
November 23, 1887 anywhere from between 30 to 300
black strikers were killed. –Stephen Kliebert

They waited till the cane had reached up
over our heads, stalks heavy with long blades,
ready for cutting, then refused as planned
by union bastards up in Pennsylvania.
Blame them for what came. It wasn't enough
what we'd lost to the North, what we paid
free negroes in scrip for our well-stocked stores—
they wanted more, but that would have cut too far
into ours, what was left us. Only guns
made them see. We forced them from the cabins
we'd provided, fortressed fields, factory, town.
Bible says don't kill, but dig anywhere
deep enough you strike blood. One of them shot
first. We stopped falling, stood, and cut them down.

Jesus Walks in Blue above Louisiana

over the jails and prisons we build for our young
dark-skinned men, two white gloves reach through
a window, finger accordion for the dancing
light-skinned crowd inside, inside the gloves the
hands are dark, outside a man stands inside night
Jesus walks in black, land so flat blue presses
down, teach us how to rise, anoint with oil
the feet and jeweled crown of Clifton Chenier
as Gabriel gives Satchmo his horn to blow
us through the whirlwind, Kingdom come, Jesus
walking on water, our feet dancing in blue
to fried catfish plate lunch, drive-through daiquiris
punch-drunk we pick a fight and hell the night
with flaming cane fields, cinders on windshields
windows shut, a/c up all year, lock out fear
fear it, talk to the dead, hoodoo spirits
spray each weed and skeeter, shoot what moves
if it flies it dies, if it lives it cries until
we rest in peace for Resurrection sealed
in vaults where this world can't ever reach us
Jesus walks in gold, gold gathers and blesses
its circle of hands while we stand outside
and curse the poor, there's oil on the water
sin in the river, cancer in the meat
and cup, the body of Jesus is sweet
he teaches us how to die.

In Isolation

I see you through the glass but you're not here

say my name your voice comes from somewhere far

where you turn and go the air receives you

what reaches me here I can't say or name

what happens names me, tells me what I've done

always the knives, blades pointing in, outside

inside my skin, I tried, try to get out

kick the thick window, my father's face, yours

feel steel hard against my fist, not nothing

not nothing, say my name, your voice a hand

I smear the glass with my food and blood so

they can't see me, plug the john, flood the floor

push my shit under the door so they'll come

take me out, take me down, bandage my wounds

say my name so I'll know I am.

Personal

To be born in this town is to dream
of getting out, only to find the doors
are few, for some a uniform
and rifle, a far desert's glare.

A german shepherd keeps throwing himself
against a chain-link fence, spinning away
to leap again, and again, snapping, snarling,
almost choking on his barks while a kid

crouches out of reach, trying to toss stones
through the chinks, as if he knows our neighbors
got the dog to guard their fear
of dark-skinned people like him.

When I ask him to stop he says, "Why?" as if
for no conceivable reason this white man
is intruding in a private matter.
He's a gangly kid, maybe fifteen,

dangling white cords feeding his ears
his personal soundtrack—
I'm background static.
He does this to everyone," I say,

which is true, but the dog keeps saying
he would eat through steel to separate
the kid's flesh from his bones,
his rage as intimate as the thick steam

of midsummer that has emptied this street
 pressing in, making it hard to breathe,
and might there not be some justice
in a perfectly thrown stone

finding the space between the beast's eyes?
"He's just a stupid-ass dog," I say,
"he doesn't know any better."
The kid turns a stone between his fingers.

"He's my friend," I hear myself lie.
The kid looks up at me as if I've just arrived.
He nods, drops the stone, turns away
and saunters off down the street

because now it's different, personal.
I watch him going, and see too late—

a friend of the dog is his enemy.
I say to no one, "But that's not *me*."

Louisiana 1 South in Winter

Drive down through Lockport and Larose,
through Cut Off and Golden Meadow,
past the signs offering live crab and crawfish,
past the shrinking towns and moldering shacks,

and the margins come to meet you—
silted water reaching up
to both sides of the two-lane,
the dulled green land scattering

into patches that seem to float
like you now, detaching
from memory—surfaces
you touch lightly passing over

as power lines step to a slow drowning,
houses lift over you on stilts,
and bridges arc in vague promises
of more than water and sky.

At road's end you arrive in Grand Isle,
not so grand, the Gulf in February gray
gnawing the shore. Here life feels storm-beaten,
clinging like the few live oaks left,

dwarfed and brittle as the seashells
shattering underfoot while you tread the edge
of what cancels and returns your eyes,
vast monotony through which summer

hurricanes gather themselves and come.
Someone in you soon turns to
go while there's still a way back.
Someone stays, staring out.

Sister of Silence and Vacant Wind

Thence retire me to my Milan, where
Every third thought shall be my grave.
--Shakespeare, The Tempest

If I drop a fork on these pine boards
the painter who lives below screams
Too loud! Too loud! from the cocoon
of Chopin, Verdi, radio hum
that wraps her solitary hours.
It's the same way her ragged voice rages
when great winds spin up out of the Gulf
to slam our walls, shake our windows.
Then she's Prospero commanding seas
or my daughter at two scolding
the tumultuous air for scattering
her magic world of sticks and paper.
I've heard a hurricane took the life
she'd created back in New Orleans,
an hour and a world away, but where
are the colleagues, friends, old lovers?—
unless vanished in the flood of years,
her every third thought turning toward her grave.
What moved her hand through unfolding
dimensions of light, color, form, leaving
images that still sing from virtual air,
from certain walls in uncertain rooms—
has it abandoned her to the silence
she tries to silence with comforting sound?
I want to have compassion, but have tired
of being so careful—my grip slipping
I keep dropping things, mocking her screech
under my breath like some grade-school kid,
her exile edging too close to my own.
Is it the vacant wind we wail against
or the place where our human powers end?

After the Chauvin Sculpture Garden

for the artist, Kenny Hill

Enter through the emptiness, when the blood
finally seeps from your chest like someone
else's, what you cannot keep, rivering
down shirt front and pant leg to puddle
between your shoes. Unroofing the sky,
two angels with re-bar wings descend
by the gate as if to help you find where
to begin this walk between the planets.

To your man of sorrows, give a seashell
and a horseshoe. Let him remember
the one angel spellbound by a butterfly
alighted in her hand. When faces appear
in the feathered, taloned columns, tell him
they're all his, not his, like the human shapes
staggering in black the trail of trials
where each footprint fits, or might, or will.

If he hauls a cross until one arm tears off
and he looks back in dismay at Yahweh
in his tower of cowboys, Indians, jazz
and Iwo Jima, following the old story
to crucifixion, may he improvise
a path beyond this palace of lost lights
and dry fountains, grabbing a great bird's legs
to lift away into further vision.

Standby

I'm possessive of my seat, still fearful
they'll call me back, give it to someone else,
leave me to face yet more lost hours
far from my final destination.
In the next row two older women
travel together. Their faces echo—
mother and daughter, maybe sisters.
The mother, gaunt, hair wispy white,
moves tentatively, as if across
a great distance opening
between herself and the world.
The daughter, hair the gray of storm clouds,
holds her mother's hand between her own,
speaks soft words through the rising roar,
kisses her cheek with affection so gentle
and unabashed, I stare and look away,
stare and look away.

*

Calmed by our ritual drinks and peanuts,
we busy ourselves with words, pictures, sounds
that tether us to the planet sliding past below,
where "Apocalyptic Blues" tops the charts.
Maybe we're safer up here, shooting through ether
in this metal tube, though now we know
how these things can be turned into missiles.

The daughter kisses her mother's cheek
again, and again, with naked love—what feels
like gratitude for a lifetime of kindness.

When the mother rises to use the toilet,
the daughter guides her down the narrow aisle,
over thinning clouds and five miles of rain-rinsed air,
June-green mountains showing through.
All fear has gone out of me.

V. What Returns

Meteor Shower

Stuttering out of black, the abundance hushed
our small talk—how they kept coming—
sparks tearing deep air, luminous
wounds closing over as quickly
as opened, gone.

Someone wondered aloud what the ancients
must have dreamed when visited by such
visions, and we spoke of omens,
imminent revelations, the end,
another beginning

as we wandered time-space in our heads,
sitting in lawn chairs, gazing, the high
desert floor arriving under our feet,
a rare clarity coming into our
voices in the dark.

I'm still trying to see them, trying to see us
there together, but you've made it hard
with your going. I'm trying to speak
as when our words
became eyes.

What Returns

To the keeper of tenantless lots,
shadows and lost names—the one who stays
through every going, returning
in what is left—I give this papery light
at winter's far margin,
I'm given blurred and lucid faces flickering
on an intermittent screen.
Uncle John, Aunt Charlotte—eternally gone!
Yet again. Four, six years? Tricks of mind—
these feet sleepwalking over vacancies
toward some vestigial heaven projected
from the private, third eye of the past.
"Don't look back," says Satchel Paige, laughing
as he leaves with Orpheus and Lot's wife.
But then the tenderness—like someone reaching
through me—when I touch the shoulder of the man
whose dog in sheer spring exuberance on her way
to the park flew from the car window,
caught her leg on the door, twisted
to somehow land under his own back tire
that crushed her skull, spilled her brain on the road.
Forever highway. Where do the dead go
but in? I follow the stains slowly
fading through asphalt skin, transparent
pages, and find a carnival starting
up in the trees, the company
of shuddering wings, dandelions
spangling dirt below an eye-searing sun.

After the Murder of an Old Friend

for T.K.

To make room for minnows
pulsing through water weeds,

for the black-and-rust-furred caterpillar
clinging to a stem.

Room for a half-moon
hatching the afternoon sky,

blue stroking my head,

that other sun
gone somewhere far.

Room for a mockingbird
on the railing a moment,

vines on the roof
of the rotting shed

coming back in green,
flowering yellow—and you

using these eyes.

A Faltering Shelter

Names and dates repeat themselves like mantras
for permanence. *Cut Flowers Will Be Removed
After Seven Days.* The green floor yields
a harvest of lasting plastic colors,
headstones and footstones growing confused—
everywhere I tread feels like trespass,
soft grass giving to my weight, I'm floating
over crumbling houses, hollowing ground.
Up the path, under arching branches
and raven profanities, a rectangle
of new sod grows crisp and pale in the dry
high desert heat: no one goes without help.
Now photographic likenesses emblazoned
on ceramic disks, fixed to gray granite—
a monument to a couple.
Between and slightly below them, the image
of Pierre, beloved poodle—buried here?
Or banished for the lack of a soul?
At the bottom, chiseled in cursive:
We Will Meet Again on the Rainbow Bridge.
Pretty words to cast a spell on space-time,
the ruinous body, reeling mind.
Yet there's something undeniable
in these faces—a disarming warmth,
generosity, remains of the fire
that first pulled them from their separate skins
flickering up from clay and nothingness.
Here was a faltering shelter that seemed
to hold the stars in place even as they burned
toward their cold. Here a bridge into the earth,
its wide circuits, the expanding air.

The Witness under Cross-Examination

You who have seen the carrion beetles swarming
inside the woodchuck's corpse, their false eyes staring up
past you at the passing clouds and what they pass through—

who have walked leafed tunnels lit by sparks pulsing, drifting
in no pattern you could discern—you know the desire
not to be changed is the strangest dream, akin

to memory's apparitions, even scenes that seem
to hold no meaning's weight: a brother and a cousin
pitching and hitting in the yard, but seen from the roof

twenty feet up, where you'd climbed to retrieve a ball,
found that different view, through thick trees the river
on its way in the distance below, curling

over the spillway to be torn in the rapids,
the soft roar so constant you'd stop hearing it
until some visitor would ask, *Is that the river?*

*

Staring at my face from a foot away,
the elderly woman seems not to see me—

I might be the stapler in her hand,
a roll of tape, scissors—any one

of the objects she's picked up and studied
as if beholding for the first time. Her eyes

register no recognition of my words
as I ask *Can I help you?* yet again,

my voice grown hard, demanding, as the room
begins to slide and sway. She reappears

nineteen, twenty years later, a spark
flaring somewhere in my erratic brain,

she stares again, I see where we stand—
a land without memory or names.

                    *

pale geckos scatter, scale
a hot brick wall, startled
up from a coolness
that didn't exist
a moment ago
in my mind

five blocks down
in the front yard of a soldier
returned from Kandahar
his disabled stepson's severed head

driving eyes combed by cane rows,
ditch banks and black water
lit by trash, white wings

clouds sliding out
of their name

in the check-out line the worry
on the young mother's pimpled face,
her boy on her hip, his brown eyes blinking
into sleep, shoes crossing smeared asphalt

palm against muscled trunk, lichen
living on bark and light

eyed, eyeless

*

Because he knows he's dying, at bedtime
the boy tells his father, *I'm afraid*
no one will remember me.

And then you're the father,
and then the son.

*

When they come I can almost
touch their shoulders almost

hear their voices without words
they welcome me into lost rooms

and fields where we sit or walk
or run as before but now

we are in no hurry
no bright knife hovers

beneath spreading branches
we listen through the distances

to the light moving in the leaves

*

Unfurling ferns, spiral galaxies,
a raccoon's handprint
blurring in the dirt.
Who is the fabulist
by a thinning window
gathering, weaving?

Whose empty hand finally opens
again, feels the current pouring through?

This Dirt Speaks

of origins, cosmic fallout still drifting
down, forty thousand tons each day mixing
with dust of stone and skin, mud, duff, clay, silt,
sediment, compost of leaf, corpse, excrement,

loam alive with our single-celled ancestors,
muck of farms we fled for dreams of freedom,
rising in skyscrapers and rockets from soil
cursed by Yahweh, dirty work, humble humus

crafting language, theories, metaphysics,
particle colliders and guitar licks,
eating what grows from dirt, eating beasts
who eat what grows from dirt, earth reaching up

through us—myriad faces, eyes—flashes
of consciousness, recognition, witness
in artifact, gesture, image, act, phrase
before we return to dirt where it waits.

As when I scraped snow from around a redbud
to pour my mother's dust on hard ground, dreaming
of magenta blossoms yet unable to foresee
the thick profusion that startled the air in spring.

Leaf

An intricate system of rivers
in a desert seen from far above,

tributaries long drained, abandoned
network of nerves inside

a scrap of hide, capillaries
and veins, lost map, brittle

piece of parchment tearing
away at the edges, inscribed

with flecks, blurrings, meanings
fled, a palm spread, fingerless, pierced

with star holes, a mask looking
back—ground

rooted

in air

a tree

trunkless

rising, leafing
throbbing veins of lightning,

green claws clasping a green branch,
thin fish dangling in a morning stream,

brushed by the slightest wind.

Where It Begins

It begins with beetles who bury
a mouse corpse to make a breeding bed,
because it begins at the end, with vultures
and ravens and maggots scouring bones,
because death feeds wings and feet, resurrects
in other names, other eyes, so I pray
with regret and gratitude to the unseen
animals who die to make meat on my plate,
who walk these legs and gaze out these eyes,
and I know that one day what I call *I*
will fill other mouths in this fire-feast
and *nothing* is ego's terror, a ghost
of consciousness, but synonym for *all.*

It begins anywhere we wake again
to light arriving from the sun where it
begins and begins like the man who stopped,
stood alone in the path of armored tanks,
like the one who turned "My Favorite Things"
inside out, blowing through seams to beyond,
like the one-armed woman who showed me
a place where love has no beginning or end,
which might be what we mean when we say
always, forever, life everlasting
with our temporal tongues.

And it begins with the blonde Labrador
when I reach over the fence, feel him quake
with joy so intense he can't bring himself
to let go the beloved ball in his mouth
which he wants to chase yet one more time
before we have to go, before night comes,
where a field opens and clocks lose count,
though the waters will rise, though the cancer

will bloom, send it seeds, the heart stammer, stop,
where singing comes from wet branches at dusk,
where exiles, refugees find welcome's door,
before the bullets, before the bomb, whence
the deathless spark, the needed words, courage,
O matter and energy in the dark.

Void

I woke to money worries, specters of bleak old age and lonely death, 3:17 a.m. I was finally nearing sleep again when I met my brother, he of the mental illness and suffering, a life without career or companion.

He was sitting at a desk, rambling as usual, conjuring lost faces and scattered scenes in extravagant detail. He was writing it all down in a checkbook as he spoke. In the two lines that begin "Pay to the Order of" and end with "Dollars," he was entering his entire life. There was no space for it, but he kept talking, writing. His eyes shone. He chuckled.

He kept writing and talking, loving the details. If he heard me, he didn't care—

Can't you see what you're doing? I demanded. *No one will take that check!*

Skinned

Arms mottled like thin shade—sun's seduction
pulled us under, old suit: such soft destruction.
What did we dream? Always you're replacing
yourself, they say, yet something of you must
always stay to remember through difference.
You shed yourself as dust, rejoin the earth,
as self can't hold itself wholly apart—
a porous border unbordering while
the guard keeps the gate. Sovereignty parades,
an occupation. I'm wrapped in my flag,
but the fabric is woven of other
stories. Mute oracle, what touch will start
the singing that seems to come from beyond
within, light through worn cloth wearing outward?

Night Rises, Seeping

from bottomless below,
in from the curved edges,

gathering in grasses,
bleeding between leaves,

slowly climbing each stem
in ditch and field—purple

clover, ghostly primrose
taken, stained by inverse rain

dissolving separate branches,
trees massing in black while

far beyond clustered buildings
the last colors wash out

to white, a final reaching
from the rim, clouds turning

to ash, quiet the tide
closing over, the blind cries,

the wide and steep surround.

Walking Home

I walked as if I went alone,
a world unto myself, a globe
balanced on two strange sticks,
but with each step the steady-
seeming earth held my dreaming
weight and carried me along.
With each unmindful breath
air came to greet my grateful lungs
and fed the blood that fed my brain
without a plan, without a thought.
The sun escorted me as if
he'd summoned these eyes into sight,
lighting and warming the way,
waiting patiently whenever
the breathing trees bathed me
in their shade, and while I slept
gravity kept me safe in my place
among the other animals
eating one another.

I knew the earthquake would come,
along with the flood, hurricane,
drought, tornado, tsunami,
wayward meteor, and then
the hot finale with that waiting star.
Still I loved the uncertain floor,
this house whose walls we've never found.

Notes on the Poems

Page 2: The italicized material in lines 5-9 is from Michael Polanyi's *Personal Knowledge*.

Page 3: The italicized material in lines 1-3 is from Temple Grandin's *Animals in Translation*.

Page 7: Drawn from the Bhagavad-Gita, "a thousand suns" and "Now I am become Death, the Destroyer of worlds" were phrases often cited by Robert Oppenheimer when recalling the first detonation of the atom bomb, at the Trinity Test Site in the New Mexico desert on July 16, 1945.

"O blessed rage for power" revises "O blessed rage for order" in Wallace Stevens' "The Idea of Order at Key West."

Page 38: "Being, but an Ear" is borrowed from the Emily Dickinson poem that begins, "I felt a Funeral, in my Brain."

Page 40: The phrase "optical delusion" and the following line are adapted from this passage by Albert Einstein: "A human being is part of the whole, called by us 'Universe' . . . He experiences himself, his thoughts and feelings as separated from the rest—a kind of optical delusion of his consciousness."

Page 43: Lines 9-10 play off the Emily Dickinson poem that begins, "Ample make this Bed—/ Make this Bed with Awe."

Page 49: Lines 18-19 refer to the practices of Abu Musab al-Zarqawi in Iraq following America's invasion in 2003.

Page 55: Line 11 references the Thibodaux Massacre of November 1887 (see the epigraph for "Strike and Harvest" on page 56). Line 12 is adapted from the song "Jambalaya," made famous by Hank Williams.

Page 57: The opening imagery draws from Michael Tisserand's recounting of the life of Amede Ardoin, the influential Creole musician, in *The Kingdom of Zydeco*. Sometimes when working house parties for whites, Ardoin would have to don white gloves and stand outside while playing his accordion through an open window.

Page 63: Line 13 echoes a favorite saying of Paige, the great baseball pitcher: "Don't look back. Something might be gaining on you."

Dedication and Thanks

This book is dedicated to Suzanne Andress-Udall, Rachel Udall, Houston Kempton, Pat Andress, Bob Jacoby, Bob and Anna Carts, Howie Faerstein, R.R. Vagnini, Craig Rosen, Priya Keefe, and all my brothers and sisters, blood and otherwise.

I would like to thank Nicholls State University for allowing me the extra time to work on these poems in my position as poet-in-residence. Thanks also to Kim Davis, David and Nancy Parsons, and the entire staff of Texas Review Press for shepherding the book home.

About the Author

Jay Udall is the author of five previous books of poetry, including *The Welcome Table*, winner of the New Mexico Book Award. He teaches at Nicholls State University in Thibodaux, Louisiana, where he also serves as poet-in-residence.

CPSIA information can be obtained
at www.ICGtesting.com
Printed in the USA
FFOW02n2237100418
46222565-47551FF

9 781680 031508